**Schwerpunktthema
Abitur Englisch**

Hanif Kureishi:
My Son the Fanatic
and Accompanying Texts

Cornelsen

Hanif Kureishi: My Son the Fanatic and Accompanying Texts

Berater
Carl Bamber, Potsdam; Paul Maloney, Hildesheim

Verlagsredaktion
Neil Porter; Bild- und Textrechte: Dr. Ilka Soennecken

Layoutkonzept
Annika Preyhs für Buchgestaltung+, Berlin

Layout und technische Umsetzung
graphitecture book & edition

Umschlaggestaltung
hawemannundmosch, Konzeption und Gestaltung, Berlin

www.cornelsen.de

1. Auflage, 3. Druck 2017

Alle Drucke dieser Auflage sind inhaltlich unverändert
und können im Unterricht nebeneinander verwendet werden.

© 2013 Cornelsen Schulverlage GmbH, Berlin
© 2017 Cornelsen Verlag GmbH, Berlin

Das Werk und seine Teile sind urheberrechtlich geschützt.
Jede Nutzung in anderen als den gesetzlich zugelassenen Fällen bedarf
der vorherigen schriftlichen Einwilligung des Verlages.
Hinweis zu den §§ 46, 52 a UrhG: Weder das Werk noch seine Teile dürfen ohne eine
solche Einwilligung eingescannt und in ein Netzwerk eingestellt oder sonst öffentlich
zugänglich gemacht werden.
Dies gilt auch für Intranets von Schulen und sonstigen Bildungseinrichtungen.

Druck: H. Heenemann, Berlin

ISBN 978-3-06-033441-4

CONTENTS

Abbreviations		3
Introduction		4
INFOBOX: Hanif Kureishi		5
1	My Son the Fanatic HANIF KUREISHI	6
2	Extremism and Muslim Extremism	15
3	Choosing between Family and God ED HUSAIN	17
4	Down with Fanatics ROGER WODDIS	22
5	Caught between Extremists on Both Sides NICK FRANCIS	23
6	Speech Following the Terrorist Attacks in London KEN LIVINGSTONE	26
7	Oppressive or Empowering? EVE AHMED	28
INFOBOX: Islam in Britain		31
Acknowledgements		32

ABBREVIATIONS

BE	British English		**p., pp.**	page, pages
adj	adjective		**pl**	plural
adv	adverb		**sing**	singular
abbr	abbreviation		**sb.**	somebody
e.g.	(Latin) exempli gratia = for example		**sl**	slang
esp.	especially		**sth.**	something
infml	informal		**usu.**	usually
jdn./jdm.	jemanden/jemandem		**v**	verb
l., ll.	line, lines		**vulg**	vulgar
n	noun			

INTRODUCTION

It is hoped that you will find working with the materials in this collection a challenge in the positive sense of the word: that you will discover motivating texts and tasks that challenge you to think, to reflect on your values and goals, and ultimately to make responsible decisions in a world that offers few certainties.

This book is centred around Hanif Kureishi's short story 'My Son the Fanatic'. Kureishi wrote the short story as a reaction to the increasing militancy of young British Muslims in the early 1990s, a trend which has continued to the present day. Kureishi first noticed this trend when Ayatollah Khomeini issued a fatwa against the British author Salman Rushdie following the publication of his novel *The Satanic Verses*. Many young British Muslims protested against the novel and supported the fatwa.
The short story concerns the fear of a secular Muslim father as he slowly realizes that his son has become an Islamist.

The idea behind this collection of texts is as follows:
- The entire class reads the short story 'My Son the Fanatic'.
- Then the 6 other texts are divided up between groups.
- Each group reads the additional text it is assigned and does the one or two allotted tasks.
- Then each group presents its text to the rest of the class. How the groups present their text is up to the group itself, but it is suggested that the texts be summarized and some form of connection between the text and 'My Son the Fanatic' be established.

The short story here is about a Muslim fundamentalist, and most of the texts reflect on various forms of fundamentalism or extremism, particularly of an Islamic nature. The reason behind the selection of this text for classroom study is that in recent times all Western countries have had to deal with the issues arising from the integration of people from different religious and ethnic backgrounds. While most Muslims are content to get on with everyday life and keep their religion a private affair, there are some who see the West as standing in opposition to Islam and reject the values of the Western countries they were brought up in. Although this book concentrates on extremists within Islam, you will see that within the texts there are all sorts of Muslims with varying views of their religion.

INFOBOX — Hanif Kureishi

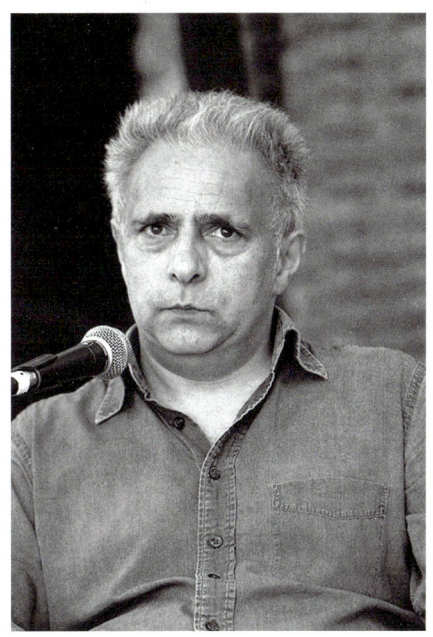

Hanif Kureishi (born 1954) was born in Bromley, in south London to a Pakistani father and an English mother. His father, Rafiushan, was from a wealthy family, most of whose members moved to Pakistan after the Partition of British India in 1947. He took a degree in philosophy at King's College, London.

He first came to public notice with his screenplay to the film *My Beautiful Laundrette* (1985), which is about a gay Pakistani-British young man and his relationship with an English skinhead.

Amongst his novels are *The Buddha of Suburbia* (1990), a semi-autobiographical novel about his relationship with his father. His novel *Intimacy* (1998) revolves around the story of a man leaving his wife and two young sons after feeling physically and emotionally rejected by his wife. It was later adapted into a successful movie.

Kureishi has also written plays and short stories, as well as non-fiction. The short story 'My Son the Fanatic' was first published in the magazine *The New Yorker* (1995) and then in his collection *Love in a Blue Time* (1997). The story was turned into a film.

Kureishi's work is often set in London and deals with social problems, especially those of immigrants and their families. Much of his work is based on his own experiences as the British-born son of a Pakistani father and a white English mother growing up in suburban London. As a lot of his work is autobiographical, his family and partners have often felt that their lives have not been fairly represented, leading to difficulties with his family. The father of the protagonist in *The Buddha of Suburbia*, for example, is based loosely on his own father. Parvez in 'My Son the Fanatic' shares some of the attitudes of the 'fictional' father in *The Buddha of Suburbia*, e.g. his love of freedom in England and his lack of respect for religious traditions.

1 My Son the Fanatic

HANIF KUREISHI

Surreptitiously, the father began going into his son's bedroom. He would sit there for hours, rousing himself only to seek clues. What bewildered him was that Ali was getting tidier. The room, which was usually a tangle of clothes, books, cricket bats and video games, was becoming neat and 5 ordered; spaces began appearing where before there had been only mess.

Initially, Parvez had been pleased: his son was outgrowing his teenage attitudes. But one day, beside the dustbin, Parvez found a torn shopping bag that contained not only old toys but computer discs, videotapes, new books and fashionable clothes the boy had bought a few months before. 10 Also without explanation, Ali had parted from the English girlfriend who used to come around to the house. His old friends stopped ringing.

For reasons he didn't himself understand, Parvez was unable to bring up the subject of Ali's unusual behaviour. He was aware that he had become slightly afraid of his son, who, between his silences, was developing a sharp 15 tongue. One remark Parvez did make – 'You don't play your guitar any more' – elicited the mysterious but conclusive reply, 'There are more important things to be done.'

Yet Parvez felt his son's eccentricity as an injustice. He had always been aware of the pitfalls that other men's sons had stumbled into in England. It 20 was for Ali that Parvez worked long hours; he spent a lot of money paying for Ali's education as an accountant. He had bought Ali good suits, all the books he required, and a computer. And now the boy was throwing his possessions out! The TV, video-player and stereo system followed the guitar. Soon the room was practically bare. Even the unhappy walls bore 25 pale marks where Ali's pictures had been removed.

Parvez couldn't sleep; he went more often to the whisky bottle, even when he was at work. He realised it was imperative to discuss the matter with someone sympathetic.

Parvez had been a taxi-driver for twenty years. Half that time he'd 30 worked for the same firm. Like him, most of the other drivers were Punjabis. They preferred to work at night, when the roads were clearer and the money better. They slept during the day, avoiding their wives. They led almost a boy's life together in the cabbies' office, playing cards and setting up practical jokes, exchanging lewd stories, eating takeaways from local 35 balti houses and discussing politics and their problems.

But Parvez had been unable to discuss the subject of Ali with his friends. He was too ashamed. And he was afraid, too, that they would blame him for the wrong turning his boy had taken, just as he had blamed other fathers whose sons began running around with bad girls, skipping 40 school and joining gangs.

For years, Parvez had boasted to the other men about how Ali excelled in cricket, swimming and football, and what an attentive scholar he was,

---

1 *surreptitious:* done secretly and quickly in the hope that other people do not notice

2 *rouse yourself* [raʊz]: become active

2 *clue:* Hinweis

2 *bewilder sb.* [bɪˈwɪldə]: puzzle sb.; confuse sb.

3 *tangle (n):* disorder

4 *bat:* Schläger

10 *part from sb.:* leave sb.; separate from sb.

11 *ring (sb.) (infml):* phone sb.

16 *elicit sth.:* (here) result in sth. (e.g. a response)

16 *conclusive:* (here) allowing for no further comment

18 *eccentricity* [ˌeksenˈtrɪsəti]: strange behaviour

19 *pitfall (usu. pl):* danger or difficulty (esp. one that is hidden and not easily seen)

19 *stumble into sth.:* fall or walk into sth. without thinking

21 *accountant:* Buchhalter/in; Rechnungsprüfer/in

27 *imperative:* absolutely necessary

28 *sympathetic:* showing understanding for sb.'s problems

31 *Punjabi:* member of an ethnic group that lives in India and Pakistan

33 *cabby (BE infml):* taxi driver

34 *practical joke:* Streich

34 *lewd* [ljuːd]: sexually rude

35 *balti:* type of Indian dish invented in Britain

38 *wrong turning:* falsche Richtung

39 *skip sth.:* miss sth. deliberately

41 *excel in sth.* [ɪkˈsel]: be very good at sth.

getting straight As in most subjects. Was it asking too much for Ali to get a good job, marry the right girl and start a family?

Once this happened, Parvez would be happy. His dreams of doing well in England would have come true. Where had he gone wrong?

One night, sitting in the taxi office on busted chairs with his two closest friends, watching a Sylvester Stallone film, Parvez broke his silence.

'I can't understand it!' he burst out. 'Everything is going from his room. And I can't talk to him any more. We were not father and son – we were brothers! Where has he gone? Why is he torturing me?' And Parvez put his head in his hands.

Even as he poured out his account, the men shook their heads and gave one another knowing glances.

'Tell me what is happening!' he demanded.

The reply was almost triumphant. They had guessed something was going wrong. Now it was clear: Ali was taking drugs and selling his possessions to pay for them. That was why his bedroom was being emptied.

'What must I do, then?'

Parvez's friends instructed him to watch Ali scrupulously and to be severe with him, before the boy went mad, overdosed or murdered someone.

Parvez staggered out into the early-morning air, terrified that they were right. His boy – the drug-addict killer!

To his relief he found Bettina sitting in his car.

Usually the last customers of the night were local 'brasses', or prostitutes. The taxi-drivers knew them well and often drove them to liaisons. At the end of the girls' night, the men would ferry them home, though sometimes they would join the cabbies for a drinking session in the office. Occasionally, the drivers would go with the girls.

'A ride in exchange for a ride,' it was called.

43 *get straight As:* get the best possible marks
47 *busted:* broken
53 *pour out sth.:* express sth. which has been hidden for a long time
53 *account (n):* story
60 *scrupulously:* very carefully
61 *severe:* strict
63 *stagger:* torkeln
64 *drug addict:* Drogensüchtige(r)
67 *liaison* [liˈeɪzn]: (here) meeting with a client to have sex
68 *ferry sb.:* (here) drive sb. to a place

Parvez and Bettina in the film version of My Son the Fanatic

Bettina had known Parvez for three years. She lived outside the town and, on the long drives home, during which she sat not in the passenger seat but beside him, Parvez had talked to her about his life and hopes, just as she talked about hers. They saw each other most nights.

He could talk to her about things he'd never be able to discuss with his own wife. Bettina, in turn, always reported on her night's activities. He liked to know where she had been and with whom.

Once, he had rescued her from a violent client, and since then they had come to care for each other.

Though Bettina had never met Ali, she heard about the boy continually. That night, when Parvez told Bettina that he suspected Ali was on drugs, to Parvez's relief, she judged neither him nor the boy, but said, 'It's all in the eyes.' They might be bloodshot; the pupils might be dilated; Ali might look tired. He could be liable to sweats, or sudden mood changes. 'OK?'

Parvez began his vigil gratefully. Now that he knew what the problem might be, he felt better. And surely, he figured, things couldn't have gone too far?

He watched each mouthful the boy took. He sat beside him at every opportunity and looked into his eyes. When he could, he took the boy's hand, checked his temperature. If the boy wasn't at home, Parvez was active, looking under the carpet, in Ali's drawers and behind the empty wardrobe – sniffing, inspecting, probing. He knew what to look for: Bettina had drawn pictures of capsules, syringes, pills, powders, rocks.

Every night, she waited to hear news of what he'd witnessed. After a few days of constant observation, Parvez was able to report that although the boy had given up sports, he seemed healthy. His eyes were clear. He didn't – as Parvez expected he might – flinch guiltily from his father's gaze. In fact, the boy seemed more alert and steady than usual: as well as being sullen, he was very watchful. He returned his father's long looks with more than a hint of criticism, of reproach, even – so much so that Parvez began to feel that it was he who was in the wrong, and not the boy.

'And there's nothing else physically different?' Bettina asked.

'No!' Parvez thought for a moment. 'But he is growing a beard.'

One night, after sitting with Bettina in an all-night coffee shop, Parvez came home particularly late. Reluctantly, he and Bettina had abandoned the drug theory, for Parvez had found nothing resembling any drug in Ali's room. Besides, Ali wasn't selling his belongings. He threw them out, gave them away or donated them to charity shops.

Standing in the hall, Parvez heard the boy's alarm clock go off.

Parvez hurried into his bedroom, where his wife, still awake, was sewing in bed. He ordered her to sit down and keep quiet, though she had neither stood up nor said a word. As she watched him curiously, he observed his son through the crack of the door.

The boy went into the bathroom to wash. When he returned to his room, Parvez sprang across the hall and set his ear at Ali's door. A muttering sound came from within. Parvez was puzzled but relieved.

84 *bloodshot:* blutunterlaufen
84 *pupil:* Pupille
84 *dilated* [daɪˈleɪtɪd]: larger than normal
85 *liable to sth.* [ˈlaɪəbl]: likely to have sth.
85 *sweat (n):* Schweißausbruch
86 *vigil:* period of observing sb./sth.
93 *sniff (v):* breathe air in through the nose in order to discover the smell of sth.
93 *probe:* examine or look for sth.
94 *syringe* [sɪˈrɪndʒ]: Spritze
94 *rock:* small hard lump (= Klumpen) in which form some drugs are sold
98 *flinch from sth.:* move away suddenly from sth.
99 *alert:* aufmerksam
100 *sullen:* silent and bad-tempered
101 *hint (n):* Spur
101 *reproach (n)* [rɪˈprəʊtʃ]: Vorwurf
106 *abandon sth.:* give up sth.; stop believing in sth.
108 *belongings (pl):* things which a person owns
109 *donate sth.:* etwas spenden
116 *mutter (v):* speak or say sth. in a quiet voice that is difficult to hear

Once this clue had been established, Parvez watched him at other times. The boy was praying. Without fail, when he was at home, he prayed five times a day.

Parvez had grown up in Lahore, where all young boys had been taught the Koran. To stop Parvez from falling asleep while he studied, the maulvi had attached a piece of string to the ceiling and tied it to Parvez's hair, so if his head fell forward, he would instantly jerk awake. After this indignity, Parvez had avoided all religions. Not that the other taxi-drivers had any more respect than he. In fact, they made jokes about the local mullahs walking around with their caps and beards, thinking they could tell people how to live, while their eyes roved over the boys and girls in their care.

Parvez described to Bettina what he had discovered. He informed the men in the taxi office. His friends, who had been so inquisitive before, now became oddly silent. They could hardly condemn the boy for his devotions.

Parvez decided to take a night off and go out with the boy. They could talk things over. He wanted to hear how things were going at college; he wanted to tell him stories about their family in Pakistan.

More than anything, he yearned to understand how Ali had discovered the 'spiritual dimension', as Bettina called it.

To Parvez's surprise, the boy refused to accompany him. He claimed he had an appointment. Parvez had to insist that no appointment could be more important than that of a son with his father.

The next day, Parvez went immediately to the street where Bettina stood in the rain wearing high heels, a short skirt and a long mac, which she would open hopefully at passing cars.

'Get in, get in!' he said.

They drove out across the moors and parked at the spot where, on better days, their view unimpeded for miles except by wild deer and horses, they'd lie back, with their eyes half-closed, saying, 'This is the life.' This time Parvez was trembling. Bettina put her arms around him.

'What's happened?'

'I've just had the worst experience of my life.'

As Bettina rubbed his head, Parvez told her that the previous evening, as he and his son had studied the menu, the waiter, whom Parvez knew, brought him his usual whisky-and-water. Parvez was so nervous he had even prepared a question. He was going to ask Ali if he was worried about his imminent exams. But first he loosened his tie, crunched a poppadum and took a long drink.

Before Parvez could speak, Ali made a face.

'Don't you know it's wrong to drink alcohol?' he had said.

'He spoke to me very harshly,' Parvez said to Bettina. 'I was about to castigate the boy for being insolent, but I managed to control myself.'

Parvez had explained patiently that for years he had worked more than ten hours a day, had few enjoyments or hobbies, and never went on holiday. Surely it wasn't a crime to have a drink when he wanted one?

---

119 *without fail:* always; without exception
121 *Lahore:* city in Pakistan
122 *maulvi* [ˈmʌlvi]: teacher of Islam
124 *jerk (v):* move suddenly
124 *indignity:* embarrassment; humiliation
126 *mullah:* teacher of Islamic religion and law
128 *rove over sb.:* (here) look at sb. with sexual interest
130 *inquisitive:* neugierig
132 *devotions:* prayers and religious practices
136 *yearn:* want sth. very much
142 *mac:* raincoat
145 *moors (pl):* high open area of land covered with rough grass that is not used for farming
146 *unimpeded:* with nothing in the way
155 *imminent:* that will happen soon
155 *crunch sth.:* eat sth. that is crispy
155 *poppadum:* thin crispy Indian bread
159 *harsh:* unkind
160 *castigate sb.:* punish sb.
160 *insolent:* rude; not polite

Parvez and Ali in the film version of My Son the Fanatic

'But it is forbidden,' the boy said.
Parvez shrugged, 'I know.'
'And so is gambling, isn't it?'
'Yes. But surely we are only human?'
Each time Parvez took a drink, the boy winced or made a fastidious face as an accompaniment. This made Parvez drink more quickly. The waiter, wanting to please his friend, brought another glass of whisky. Parvez knew he was getting drunk, but he couldn't stop himself. Ali had a horrible look, full of disgust and censure. It was as if he hated his father.

Halfway through the meal, Parvez suddenly lost his temper and threw a plate on the floor. He felt like ripping the cloth from the table, but the waiters and other customers were staring at him. Yet he wouldn't stand for his own son's telling him the difference between right and wrong. He knew he wasn't a bad man. He had a conscience.

There were a few things of which he was ashamed, but on the whole he had lived a decent life.

'When have I had time to be wicked?' he asked Ali.

In a low monotonous voice the boy explained that Parvez had not, in fact, lived a good life. He had broken countless rules of the Koran.

'For instance?' Parvez demanded.

Ali didn't need to think. As if he had been waiting for this moment, he asked his father if he didn't relish pork pies.

'Well.' Parvez couldn't deny that he loved crispy bacon smothered with mushrooms and mustard and sandwiched between slices of fried bread. In fact, he ate this for breakfast every morning.

Ali then reminded Parvez that he had ordered his wife to cook pork sausages, saying to her, 'You're not in the village now. This is England. We have to fit in.'

168 *wince:* (zusammen-)zucken
168 *fastidious:* (here) showing disgust
169 *accompaniment:* (hier) Begleiterscheinung
172 *censure (n):* strong criticism
175 *not stand for sth.:* not let sb. do sth.; not let sth. happen
179 *decent* ['diːsənt]: honest and fair
185 *relish sth.:* enjoy sth. very much
185 *pork pie:* Schweinefleischpastete
186 *smother sth.:* cover sth. thickly
187 *sandwich sth.:* fit or put sth. between two other things (esp. bread)

Parvez was so annoyed and perplexed by this attack that he called for more drink.

'The problem is this,' the boy said. He leaned across the table. For the first time that night his eyes were alive. 'You are too implicated in Western civilisation.'

Parvez burped; he thought he was going to choke. 'Implicated!' he said. 'But we live here!'

'The Western materialists hate us,' Ali said. 'Papa, how can you love something which hates you?'

'What is the answer, then,' Parvez said miserably, 'according to you?'

Ali didn't need to think. He addressed his father fluently, as if Parvez were a rowdy crowd which had to be quelled or convinced.

The law of Islam would rule the world; the skin of the infidel would burn off again and again; the Jews and Christers would be routed. The West was a sink of hypocrites, adulterers, homosexuals, drug users and prostitutes.

While Ali talked, Parvez looked out the window as if to check that they were still in England.

'My people have taken enough. If the persecution doesn't stop, there will be jihad. I, and millions of others, will gladly give our lives for the cause.'

'But why, why?' Parvez said.

'For us, the reward will be in Paradise.'

'Paradise!'

Finally, as Parvez's eyes filled with tears, the boy urged him to mend his ways.

'But how would that be possible?' Parvez asked.

'Pray,' urged Ali. 'Pray beside me.'

Parvez paid the bill and ushered his boy out of there as soon as he was able. He couldn't take any more.

Ali sounded as if he'd swallowed someone else's voice.

On the way home, the boy sat in the back of the taxi, as if he were a customer. 'What has made you like this?' Parvez asked him, afraid that somehow he was to blame for all this. 'Is there a particular event which has influenced you?'

'Living in this country.'

'But I love England,' Parvez said, watching his boy in the rear-view mirror. 'They let you do almost anything here.'

'That is the problem,' Ali replied.

For the first time in years, Parvez couldn't see straight. He knocked the side of the car against a lorry, ripping off the wing mirror. They were lucky not to have been stopped by the police: Parvez would have lost his licence and his job.

Back at the house, as he got out of the car, Parvez stumbled and fell in the road, scraping his hands and ripping his trousers. He managed to haul himself up. The boy didn't even offer him his hand.

195 *implicated:* involved in sth. that is criminal

197 *burp (v):* rülpsen

197 *choke:* ersticken

203 *rowdy:* noisy and disorderly

203 *quell sth.:* (here) quieten sth.

204 *infidel* ['ɪnfɪdəl]: non-believer

205 *Christer* ['kraɪstə] *(derog):* Christian

205 *rout sb.* [raʊt]: destroy sb.

206 *sink:* Ausguss

206 *adulterer* [ə'dʌltərə]: Ehebrecher/in

210 *persecution:* Verfolgung

211 *jihad:* (in Islam) holy war

216 *urge sb. to do sth.:* try hard to persuade sb. to do sth.

216 *mend your ways:* change or improve your lifestyle

220 *usher sb.:* lead sb. (usu. quickly and forcefully)

236 *scrape sth.:* die Haut von etwas abschürfen

236 *haul sb./sth.:* pull sb./sth.

Parvez told Bettina he was willing to pray, if that was what the boy wanted – if it would dislodge the pitiless look from his eyes. 'But what I object to,' he said, 'is being told by my own son that I am going to Hell!'

What had finished Parvez off was the boy's saying he was giving up his studies in accounting. When Parvez had asked why, Ali said sarcastically that it was obvious. 'Western education cultivates an anti-religious attitude.' And in the world of accountants it was usual to meet women, drink alcohol and practise usury.

'But it's well-paid work,' Parvez argued. 'For years you've been preparing!'

Ali said he was going to begin to work in prisons, with poor Muslims who were struggling to maintain their purity in the face of corruption. Finally, at the end of the evening, as Ali went up to bed, he had asked his father why he didn't have a beard, or at least a moustache.

'I feel as if I've lost my son,' Parvez told Bettina. 'I can't bear to be looked at as if I'm a criminal. I've decided what to do.'

'What is it?'

'I'm going to tell him to pick up his prayer mat and get out of my house. It will be the hardest thing I've ever done, but tonight I'm going to do it.'

'But you mustn't give up on him,' said Bettina. 'Many young people fall into cults and superstitious groups. It doesn't mean they'll always feel the same way.' She said Parvez had to stick by his boy.

Parvez was persuaded that she was right, even though he didn't feel like giving his son more love when he had hardly been thanked for all he had already given.

For the next two weeks, Parvez tried to endure his son's looks and reproaches. He attempted to make conversation about Ali's beliefs.

But if Parvez ventured any criticism, Ali always had a brusque reply.

On one occasion, Ali accused Parvez of 'grovelling' to the whites; in contrast, he explained, he was not 'inferior'; there was more to the world than the West, though the West always thought it was best.

'How is it you know that?' Parvez said. 'Seeing as you've never left England?'

Ali replied with a look of contempt.

One night, having ensured there was no alcohol on his breath, Parvez sat down at the kitchen table with Ali. He hoped Ali would compliment him on the beard he was growing, but Ali didn't appear to notice it.

The previous day, Parvez had been telling Bettina that he thought people in the West sometimes felt inwardly empty and that people needed a philosophy to live by.

'Yes,' Bettina had said. 'That's the answer. You must tell him what your philosophy of life is. Then he will understand that there are other beliefs.'

After some fatiguing consideration, Parvez was ready to begin. The boy watched him as if he expected nothing.

Haltingly, Parvez said that people had to treat one another with respect, particularly children their parents. This did seem, for a moment, to affect the boy. Heartened, Parvez continued. In his view, this life was all there

239 *dislodge sth.:* make sth. go away

245 *usury* ['juːʒəri]: practice of lending money at very high interest rates

257 *superstitious:* abergläubisch

262 *endure sth.:* bear sth.

264 *venture sth.:* attempt to put forward sth.; suggest sth.

265 *grovel to sb.:* behave with too much respect to sb.

268 *seeing as:* since; because of the fact that

270 *contempt:* Verachtung

279 *fatiguing (adj):* tiring

281 *halting:* stopping and starting often, esp. because you are not certain or are not very confident

283 *heartened:* feeling more hopeful

was, and when you died, you rotted in the earth. 'Grass and flowers will grow out of my grave, but something of me will live on.'

'How then?'

'In other people. For instance, I will continue – in you.'

At this the boy appeared a little distressed.

'And in your grandchildren,' Parvez added for good measure. 'But while I am here on earth I want to make the best of it. And I want you to, as well!'

'What d'you mean by "make the best of it"?' asked the boy.

'Well,' said Parvez. 'For a start … you should enjoy yourself. Yes. Enjoy yourself without hurting others.'

Ali said that enjoyment was a 'bottomless pit'.

'But I don't mean enjoyment like that,' said Parvez. 'I mean the beauty of living.'

'All over the world our people are oppressed,' was the boy's reply.

'I know,' Parvez replied, not entirely sure who 'our people' were, 'but still – life is for living!'

Ali said, 'Real morality has existed for hundreds of years. Around the world millions and millions of people share my beliefs. Are you saying you are right and they are all wrong?' Ali looked at his father with such aggressive confidence that Parvez would say no more.

A few evenings later, Bettina was riding in Parvez's car after visiting a client when they passed a boy on the street.

'That's my son,' Parvez said, his face set hard. They were on the other side of town, in a poor district, where there were two mosques.

Bettina turned to see. 'Slow down then, slow down!'

She said, 'He's good-looking. Reminds me of you. But with a more determined face. Please, can't we stop?'

'What for?'

'I'd like to talk to him.'

Parvez turned the cab round and stopped beside the boy.

'Coming home?' Parvez asked. 'It's quite a way.'

The boy shrugged and got into the back seat. Bettina sat in the front. Parvez became aware of Bettina's short skirt, her gaudy rings and ice-blue eyeshadow. He became conscious that the smell of her perfume, which he loved, filled the cab. He opened the window.

While Parvez drove as fast as he could, Bettina said gently to Ali, 'Where have you been?'

'The mosque,' he said.

'And how are you getting on at college? Are you working hard?'

'Who are you to ask me these questions?' he said, looking out of the window. Then they hit bad traffic, and the car came to a standstill.

By now, Bettina had inadvertently laid her hand on Parvez's shoulder. She said, 'Your father, who is a good man, is very worried about you. You know he loves you more than his own life.'

'You say he loves me,' the boy said.

'Yes!' said Bettina.

294 *bottomless pit:* (hier) bodenloser Abgrund

316 *gaudy* ['gɔːdi]: cheap and in bad taste

325 *inadvertently:* without thinking; without noticing

MY SON THE FANATIC

'Then why is he letting a woman like you touch him like that?'

If Bettina looked at the boy in anger, he looked back at her with cold fury.

She said, 'What kind of woman am I that deserves to be spoken to like that?'

'You know what kind,' he said. Then he turned to his father. 'Now let me out.'

'Never,' Parvez replied.

'Don't worry, I'm getting out,' Bettina said.

'No, don't!' said Parvez. But even as the car moved forward, she opened the door and threw herself out – she had done this before – and ran away across the road. Parvez stopped and shouted after her several times, but she had gone.

Parvez took Ali back to the house, saying nothing more to him. Ali went straight to his room. Parvez was unable to read the paper, watch television or even sit down. He kept pouring himself drinks.

At last, he went upstairs and paced up and down outside Ali's room. When, finally, he opened the door, Ali was praying. The boy didn't even glance his way.

Parvez kicked him over. Then he dragged the boy up by the front of his shirt and hit him. The boy fell back. Parvez hit him again. The boy's face was bloody. Parvez was panting; he knew that the boy was unreachable, but he struck him none the less. The boy neither covered himself nor retaliated; there was no fear in his eyes. He only said, through his split lip: 'So who's the fanatic now?'

351 *pant (v):* breathe quickly
352 *retaliate:* fight back

1. How did you react to the last paragraph of the story?

2. Examine the conflict as it develops in the story between father and son. Use a chart to show the development.

3. Write a character description of Parvez.

4. Examine the role of Bettina in the story. Take into consideration what she represents for Parvez and for Ali.

5. Role-play:
Write and act out a scene between Bettina and Ali's English girlfriend (cf. l. 6) in which they share their experiences of Ali's change in character.

2 Extremism and Muslim Extremism

eHow is a website that attempts to provide answers to all sorts of questions. Here is what it says about extremism in general and Muslim extremism in particular.

Extremism
According to the Oxford English Dictionary, an extremist is a person 'disposed to go to the extreme, or who holds extreme opinions'. This means that an extremist is a person whose beliefs or actions are beyond the bounds of what is considered normal or moral behavior.

The idea of extremism is often linked to politics. Adolf Hitler is one example. However, a person who believes in running to the point of physical collapse could also be considered an extremist, since her actions are likely to be considered excessive and unhealthy. The word 'extremist' almost always has a negative connotation.

A person so strongly opposed to abortion that he would blow up a clinic is likely to be an extremist; so is a person willing to commit a suicide bombing because of her opposition to a foreign army.

Theorists such as David Hume and Eric Hoffer have tried to pinpoint the factors that cause people to partake in politically-motivated violence. Both emphasize the idea that individuals who commit violent acts for a cause come from environments where there is social stress and deliberately-fostered hatred. Their research implies that extremism and/or fanaticism can be deliberately cultivated for larger political or religious reasons.

In his book *The True Believer* Eric Hoffer also theorized that people are attracted to extremist social movements because of certain personality characteristics: they feel powerless, flawed or insecure. According to Hoffer, joining a political or religious cause allows these people to feel a sense of belonging and pride. Subsequent theorists have agreed. Annette Schaefer has emphasized the fact that terrorists are not simply mentally ill individuals but people who want to take part in a larger group identity. [...]

Different Types of Religious Muslims
News reports and politicians don't always distinguish between groups of Muslims who are seeking to violently seize power of a particular country, those who seek power by democratic means, those who use violence in the quest for global dominance and those whose ideas about religion seem archaic, but who have little interest in politics or violence. These groups can be completely opposed to each other's aims, and conflating them makes it harder to fight those who are a true threat. Recognizing that the groups who plan attacks on American or British airplanes are not the same as those who are religiously conservative is key to working towards global security.

Fundamentalism is a religious view that sees the past as better than the present, and promotes the idea that a way of life is under attack by the modern world. Groups like the Salafiyyah and Tablighi Jamaat seek to

3 *disposed to do sth.:* willing or likely to do sth.

5 *bounds:* limits

14 *pinpoint sth.:* discover the exact facts about sth.

15 *partake in sth.:* take part in sth.

17 *deliberately-fostered:* that is encouraged for a reason

22 *flawed:* not perfect

31 *quest:* search

33 *conflate sth.:* mix sth. up with another thing

return to a purer time, and may adopt a strict dress code. They encourage women to be homemakers and limit contact with men, and are vigilant about worship and imitating the Prophet Muhammad and his contemporaries. While they sometimes have sympathy for jihadists or Islamists, their participation in any quest for political power is low.

Defining Islamism
Islamists are those who seek political power to create a theocratic state. This may be done by force, like the Taliban, by influencing public opinion, like the international Hizb ut-Tahrir, or by democratic means, like Hamas in Gaza. Their aims are usually focused on one country. Islamists believe that a theocratic government can resolve the social and economic problems their countries face. They believe that Islam will help them create the ideal society. Reza Aslan believes that this makes these groups a more manageable concern, as he explains in his 'How to Win a Cosmic War' that groups like Hezbollah want political control of a definable area, which is much easier to negotiate with than the aims of al-Qaida, which is classified as a jihadist group.

About Jihadism
Jihadism is a term derived from the word jihad, which means to strive. It has never been interpreted by traditional Islamic scholars to mean a war of aggression. Al-Qaida blindsided traditional Islamic scholars by taking the term jihad for their acts of aggression. They claim greater authenticity than traditional Islamic scholars. While Anwar al-Awlaki is formally trained in religion and was a mainstream Islamic scholar, jihadism is the brainchild of Osama bin Laden and Ayman al-Zawahiri, neither of whom received religious training beyond the elementary level.

Jihadism bills itself as the purest form of Islam. However, jihadism is an ideology of opportunism. Islamic source texts forbid suicide, attacking non-combatants and initiating violence against Muslims. These condemnations are circumvented by claiming a need that overrides these prohibitions.

Jihadists are engaged in a cosmic battle – a battle between the ideas of good and evil itself. The former, to them, consists of those who agree with them; the latter consists of those who disagree with them, no matter their faith.

---

55 *definable:* that can be described exactly
61 *blindside sb.:* surprise sb., usu. with harmful results
67 *bill yourself as sth.:* present yourself as sth. (even if it is not true)
68 *source text:* (here) text which provides the information on which a religion is based
69 *condemnation:* forbidding of sth. under severe penalty
70 *override sth.:* take a decision not to obey sth. because you have more authority
74 *no matter:* egal

---

1 Having read about Ali in 'My Son the Fanatic', explain which parts of this text might be relevant to his character.

2 Summarize each of the sections of the text in one sentence.

3 EXTRA:
List all the Arabic names in the text. Do research on each.

3 Choosing between Family and God

ED HUSAIN

Ed Husain

Mohamed Mahbub Husain (more often referred to as Ed Husain) was born to a Bangladeshi Muslim family in 1974 in the East End of London. His parents followed a spiritual form of Islam based on Sufi traditions, led by a guru, who Hussein called Grandpa (cf. l. 68). As a teenager he felt attracted to the more militant groups of Islam and started to go to the meetings of the YMO (Youth Muslim Organization).

Towards the end of summer 1991 I started to say my dawn prayers in congregation at the mosque in Stepney. I would wake up before sunrise, prepare for prayers and walk over to the mosque. There were about seven of us activists who prayed at the mosque, but there was more to our presence than prayers. We were never content with merely praying – we had more to do.

After most people had left, Sami, the university student who had taught us that democracy started with Muslim caliphs, would deliver lessons from the Koran. For about thirty minutes after the morning prayer, half asleep, I sat and listened to his impromptu commentary on the Koran. The idea behind such early-morning study sessions was to establish a YMO presence in the mosque and, gradually, win acceptance of the elderly congregation. That way, recruiting their sons to the YMO through public events at the mosque would be easier.

While I targeted others' children, all was not well at my own home. My parents were becoming seriously concerned about my sudden outburst of religious fervour. Even in a pious family like ours my behavior was at odds with my parents' faith. My father wondered what drove me to walk so far, so early in the morning. Was it merely to pray? Surely, God was at home, too. My God, however, was no longer at home; he had to be sought out in activism, drive, mobilizing and expanding the Islamic movement. I had to be a 'true Muslim', completely enmeshed in Islam, not a 'partial Muslim' like my parents.

While I supported this new endeavor of YMO to expand seriously beyond our East London stronghold, there were others who were watching me. The then imam of the mosque in Stepney was a disciple of Grandpa. I had assumed that he had forgotten me, a face among so many faces who had surrounded an elderly frail Muslim scholar. I was wrong.

The imam remembered me. He tried to make eye contact with me several times, while I sat among the YMO members. As with most mosques in Britain, imams, sadly, tend to be meek. They are bullied by the all-powerful mosque committees with their loud-mouthed chairman, and are dependent on the congregational collections for their meagre incomes. As

2 *congregation:* group of people who gather together to worship God
8 *caliph:* (formerly) the leader of the Muslim world or area
10 *impromptu:* done without preparation
17 *fervour:* very strong feelings
17 *pious:* fromm
17 *be at odds with sb./sth.:* be different from sb./sth. so that conflict results
20 *seek out sth. (sought – sought):* look for sth.
22 *enmeshed:* totally involved in sth.
26 *then:* damalig
28 *frail:* weak
31 *meek:* sanftmütig
33 *meagre* ['miːgə]: small

18 CHOOSING BETWEEN FAMILY AND GOD

such, and contrary to popular opinion, with a small number of exceptions imams very rarely rock the boat. The YMO were perceived in Stepney as a well-connected, well-organized, educated group of young men, outside the domain of a mosque imam. He humbly led the prayers, then left us to listen to the lectures of Sami. It never occurred to us that if it was genuine knowledge we sought, it should have been the imam, the person who had studied Islam, to whom we should be listening, not an undergraduate.

My parents knew that the time for GCSE revision had long passed, but still I went to the East London mosque with Falik. This was of real concern to my father, but he was waiting for the right moment to ask me what I was actually doing. Sensing his deep unease, I tried to avoid him as much as possible in the evenings; I kept myself away from the dinner table, locked inside my bedroom, citing all sorts of excuses.

In the past I had always enjoyed spending time with my parents. If I went out I always told them where I was going and when I returned, the first thing I did was to tell them I was home. Now I was desperate to change that. I did not want my mother to know when I left, where I went, or how long I stayed out. That way I could spend more time at East London mosque without having to explain myself. My strange conduct worried my parents.

One Saturday […] I was sitting in the main hall of the mosque, late in the evening, among a group of sixty or so activists when suddenly the mosque caretaker, Mr Khan, popularly known as Khan sahib, walked into the hall, his large bunch of keys jingling on his waist loops. I looked up to see him walking across the hall, more slowly than usual, and looking straight at me. He raised his arm discreetly and pointed to the main doors behind him that led to the prayer hall.

There, in the distance, stood my father with his hands in his pockets, his face long and wary, his eyes fixed on me, the son he had now lost. My heart was pounding. I froze, unable to move or say anything. Before others could notice, my father turned round and disappeared. As I saw him walk away, I knew that was the end: I had abandoned him, destroyed any hope he had had of raising a decent Muslim son. Khan sahib came up to me and tried to make conversation but I was elsewhere, in my father's mind. All those moments he had spent, training me at Grandpa's feet, had come to naught. I knew my father's hurt was deep.

That night I lost my sturdy confidence among my fellow activists. I was sad and desolate at knowing, feeling, my father's pain. Several YMO members tried to comfort me.

'This is one way God tests his servants,' said one. 'Your parents will be an obstacle to your commitment to God's work, the Islamist movement. Ours is the work of prophets, and they were opposed by their families. Abraham was rejected by his family. And in turn Abraham rejected his father.'

Another said, 'Partial Muslims like our parents will never understand what we are trying to do. Be patient, brother. You are from among true Muslims.'

35 *rock the boat:* upset a situation
35 *perceive sb./sth.:* view sb./sth.
37 *domain:* area of control
37 *humble:* bescheiden
41 *GCSE:* exams taken at age 16
44 *sense sth.:* feel sth.
44 *unease* [ʌnˈiːz]: feeling of being worried or unhappy about sth.
46 *cite sth.:* mention sth. as a reason
56 *sahib (Bengali):* mister
57 *loops:* rings on trousers which a belt goes through
62 *wary* [ˈweəri]: cautious, uncertain
63 *pound:* beat fast
69 *naught* [nɔːt]: nothing
70 *sturdy:* strong, certain
71 *desolate:* lost, miserable

They were wrong, I thought. My parents were different: overly protective, exceptionally caring, and committed to God as much as, if not more than, those who claimed to be doing the work of the prophets. Those arguments did not wash with me. These were difficult moments, yes, but not a test from God. Still, I decided to be patient.

As time passed, my parents and I were hardly on speaking terms. I continued to spend long hours in my GCSEs. Uneasy about my involvement in Islamism, relatives advised my parents that perhaps I ought to be sent off to work in an Indian restaurant far away from East London mosque.

My parents, though, wanted me to continue studying, and my father wanted me to resit my exams at Tower Hamlets College. However, he also wanted a promise that I would study and not spend my time with YMO or visit the East London mosque. It was a promise I could not make, for deep down I had committed myself, my life, to the Islamist movement and, like my brothers at the mosque, I would let nothing stand in the way of following Islam as a complete life code. My father and I engaged in long hours of heated debate about the nature of Islam. [...]

I tried to answer his questions but he was in no mood to be taught lessons from his son. I tried to explain to him that Islam had been misunderstood by most of the people he knew. I dared not mention Grandpa in this context. Noticing my newly developed confrontational attitude, both my parents look on, stupefied.

'You've changed,' my mother said, her lips quivering. 'You're no longer the son I raised.' I wanted to hear no more. Abruptly, I got up and walked out of the living room. My parents shouted at me; never in my life had I walked away from my parents while they were speaking to me.

They were both vehemently opposed to my version of Islam and made their dissatisfaction in no uncertain terms. My father spent long hours trying to explain that Islam was spiritual, internal, and about drawing closer to God and not about radical politics, assassinating politicians and trying to set up an imaginary Islamic state. 'If you want politics,' he would say, 'go and join the Labour Party.' But British politics was man-made and I was aspiring to a politics that was God-made.

And so I continued to attend events at East London mosque while studying to resit my exams. I raised money for the mosque on Fridays, regularly helped the caretaker with small tasks, and, most importantly, started to help Sami set up a library in the mosque. We spent hours sifting through cartons of books we received from an American high school, and others from Muslim publishers. This was our attempt to create a more studious environment for our brothers.

The atmosphere at home was horrid. In January 1992, when I was seventeen, I minimized my involvement with YMO for a two-month period in an attempt at conciliation. I wanted to regain some of that old warmth and love my parents had showered on me, but I did not want to lose my brothers, my friends at East London mosque. Falik was now studying with me at Tower Hamlets College and he kept me up to date with events at the

81 *overly:* too; too much
92 *resit sth.:* take sth. (esp. an exam) again
98 *heated:* full of anger and emotion
103 *stupefied* ['stjuːpɪfaɪd]: shocked
114 *aspire to sth.:* have a strong desire to achieve sth.

mosque. I still maintained my daily routine sheet, and read bulletins issued by Jamat-e-Islami. [...]

That summer my father saw on my desk at home a pile of the leaflets I had been handing out. As far as my father was concerned, that was the last straw. He had seen me drift further and further away from the family; he had spent hours trying to engage with me, explain to me that Islam was not politics, but about purifying our hearts and drawing closer to God.

He was shaking with anger.

'What is Gulkam Azam doing in my house?' he shouted, before launching into a monologue about the Islamists, their shrewd manipulation of religion to suit their political needs, their hatred of traditional Muslims, and their disregard for Muslim saints. He called them 'the enemies of the Prophet, the cursed of God, allies of the devil, and the rejects of the Muslims. From this day onwards, you will have nothing to do with them! Enough! Enough of pretending to study, then lying to us, deceiving us ...'

He slammed the door and left. My mother stood in the room alone with me and wept profusely, repeatedly asking in a broken, shaking voice, 'Why? Why?'

My disagreements with my parents were now so deep, their revulsion for my Islamism so powerful, and my commitment to ideological Islam so uncompromising, that my father had little choice but to give me an ultimatum: leave Mawdudi's Islamism or leave my house.

'We raised you as a Muslim, you understand Islam. If you want to stay under my roof, then you will be a normal Muslim, none of this politics in the name of religion.'

I turned to my friends in YMO for advice and they told me again that this was a test from God.

'You must choose between family and God's work. The Islamic movement is more important to us than our families,' said a leading member of YMO.

My father continued to apply pressure on me. He was worried that I would be a negative influence on my siblings. All the while my friends in the Islamic movement were critical of my parents, suggesting that they were not true Muslims. Only those who accepted Mawdudi and his Egyptian counterpart, Syed Qutb, understood 'true Islam'.

Unable to accept two authorities, one night, late in the summer, I wrote a farewell note to my parents, left it on my pillow and crept out of our house while they slept. I left home for the Islamic movement without a penny in my pocket and with only the clothes I was wearing.

129 *Jamat-e-Islami:* Pakistani Islamist party

134 *purify sth.:* make sth. spiritually clean

136 *Gulkam Azam:* Bangladeshi Islamist leader

150 *Mawdudi:* Pakistani Islamist leader

159 *apply sth.:* put sth.

163 *Syed Qutb* [ˈsæiːd ˈkʊtuːb]: Egyptian Islamist who was a leading member of the Muslim Brotherhood

CHOOSING BETWEEN FAMILY AND GOD **21**

1 Complete the table below by finding extracts from 'My Son the Fanatic' that resemble Ed Husain's account.

My Son the Fanatic	Ed's story
For reasons he didn't himself understand, Parvez was unable to bring up the subject of Ali's unusual behaviour. He was aware that he had become slightly afraid of his son, who, between his silences, was developing a sharp tongue.	
In a low monotonous voice the boy explained that Parvez had not, in fact, lived a good life. He had broken countless rules of the Koran.	
For the next two weeks, Parvez tried to endure his son's looks and reproaches. He attempted to make conversation about Ali's beliefs.	
'I feel as if I've lost my son,' Parvez told Bettina.	
Ali said, 'Real morality has existed for hundreds of years. Around the world millions and millions of people share my beliefs. Are you saying you are right and they are all wrong?'	
Haltingly, Parvez said that people had to treat one another with respect, particularly children their parents. This did seem, for a moment, to affect the boy.	
'I'm going to tell him to pick up his prayer mat and get out of my house. It will be the hardest thing I've ever done, but tonight I'm going to do it.'	

2 Role-play:
  Imagine Ed's father meets Parvez. Write down and act out a dialogue as they share their experiences and suggest ways forward.

4 Down with Fanatics

ROGER WODDIS

If I had my way with violent men
I'd simmer them in oil,
I'd fill a pot with bitumen
And bring them to the boil.
I'd execrate the terrorist
And those who harbour him,
And if I weren't a moralist
I'd tear them limb from limb.

Fanatics are an evil breed
Whom decent men should shun;
I'd like to flog them till they bleed,
Yes, every mother's son,
I'd like to tie them to a board
And let them taste the cat,
While giving praise, oh thank the Lord,
That I am not like that.

For we should love the human kind,
As Jesus taught us to,
And those who don't should be struck blind
And beaten black and blue;
I'd like to roast them in a grill
And listen to them shriek,
Then break them on the wheel until
They turned the other cheek.

---

2 *simmer sth.:* boil sth. gently
3 *bitumen* ['bɪtʃʊmɪn]: black sticky substance used on roads or roofs
5 *execrate sb.:* curse sb.
6 *harbour sb.:* hide and shelter sb.
9 *breed:* type of person
10 *shun sb.:* avoid sb.
14 *cat = cat-o'-nine-tails:* whip with nine cords used formerly to punish prisoners
23 *break sb. on the wheel:* jdn. aufs Rad flechten

1 a) Discuss in groups of three or four the speaker's attitude towards fanatics. Consider the title of the poem and the means the speaker would use to fight fanatics in your discussion.
  b) Now formulate the poet's attitude to fanatics and fanaticism.

2 Explain how the poem relates to the short story.

5 Caught between Extremists on Two Sides
NICK FRANCIS

Britain is often seen as an example of a successful multicultural society, in which different religions and ethnic groups live side by side. But sometimes different values can result in tension, as is shown in this article from the popular tabloid The Sun.

Nestled in the rolling Bedfordshire countryside, Luton was once a gleaming advert for prosperous Britain. Over the centuries it grew as an international centre for hat making before exploding in size when the Vauxhall car plant opened in 1905.

But today, Luton has become synonymous with something to be far less proud of – race hate and intolerance.

The town is 15 per cent Muslim – five times the national average – and is an epicentre of both radical Islam and far-Right racism. It is a hotbed of fundamental Muslim groups [...].

But growing like an equally aggressive cancer in its heart is the English Defence League, headed by Tommy Robinson. [...] The EDL was spawned after Muslim protesters screamed 'rapist' and 'murderers' at our war-weary troops during a homecoming for the Royal Anglian Regiment in Luton in March 2009. In January 2010, five men charged over the bile-filled attack were given conditional discharges, something that didn't sit well with Robinson.

'It wasn't so much the fact that they did it,' he says. 'It was the fact they were allowed to do it. The EDL aren't racist, Islam isn't a race, it's a religion. We are anti-Islam.

'If I was put in power tomorrow the first thing I'd do is stop any more Muslims coming into the country. I would keep a ban on them until Islam learns to integrate with British society.'

Without flinching, Robinson makes wildly inflammatory statements. 'If we don't do anything about it we'll have the same troubles we had with Northern Ireland, but worse. This country is just three per cent Muslim and look at the chaos they're causing already.'

He claims to have read the Koran, cherry picking facts to prop up his case. 'If you take Islam literally it is aggressive, preaches non-tolerance of other religions. It is anti-Semitic and homophobic. This country will be ruined within 20 years if we don't do something.'

Walking around Luton with Robinson offers a snapshot of a town polarised by resentment. Within seconds a young Asian man shouted at him: 'What the f*** are you looking at you ****?'

Robinson spat back: 'You're the one looking at me you p***k.'

Elsewhere people cheered Robinson's name and patted him on the back. A bunch of teenage girls, two of them black, began chanting 'EDL, EDL.'

1 *nestled:* located between hills
1 *gleaming:* shining
8 *hotbed:* Brutstätte
11 *spawn sth.:* cause sth. to develop
13 *homecoming:* parade for soldiers when they return from abroad
14 *bile-filled:* full of hatred
15 *conditional discharge:* sentence in which the offender receives no punishment provided that, in a period set by the court, no further offence is committed
23 *flinch:* show emotion
32 *resentment:* Groll

Although Robinson dreams of a day when the EDL are a recognised political party, he reminds us why this can never happen. 'If you gave me the address of (*hate preacher*) Abu Qatada I'd be there tomorrow with 200 lads. He'd soon leave after we've finished with him.'

The 29-year-old is a trained aircraft engineer and plumber, yet since his EDL activities he is virtually unemployable. He runs a tanning salon to support his wife and three kids.

He says: 'I can't get a job. My family hate me doing this. At rallies, when we march through Muslim areas, I have to wear a stab vest. I did this because I believe in it.'

In Channel 4 documentary 'Proud And Prejudiced', aired tonight at 10pm, Robinson is followed by cameras for a year. He is seen fighting with his own followers after they booed a Sikh man joining the group, throwing coins at police on a night out and getting death threats on the phone during a rally.

Also on the documentary is Saiful Islam, also from Luton, who represents everything Robinson says he hates. Saiful is a disciple of exiled extremist Omar Bakri and a founder of Al-Muhajiroun, a group banned for glorification of terrorism. It is Saiful's mission to overthrow the Government and impose Sharia law in the UK, which he says will solve many of the country's problems.

At a meeting secretly filmed by *The Sun* last year, Saiful was recorded ranting: 'The blame of 9/11 belongs to no one but the American government. They are the terrorists.'

In the documentary, Saiful is seen punching Robinson through an open car window — an act he says he regrets.

'I did it out of frustration,' says Saiful, 32. 'He wouldn't listen to me and was driving away. He is a racist. I don't hate the EDL, they are just ignorant, uneducated.'

In Luton, Saiful and his band of followers aren't allowed into most mosques and are denounced by moderate Muslims. He preaches on the streets of Bury Park. 'People misunderstand Sharia law,' he says. 'They focus on the stories of women being beaten or thieves having their hands cut off. That's not what it's about.

'The system in Britain is failing. There are many problems of drug addiction, prostitution, alcoholism. Sharia would end all of this. Sharia is about helping the citizens – everybody would be clothed and fed, kept warm. There would be an end to drug addiction as drugs would be kept out. There would be no pubs or bars and no lives ruined by drink. We would ban it. Open homosexuality would be banned too, as well as prostitution. Women would not be allowed to dress the way they do. [...] This would end all the problems that come from sexualisation of women. Britain has the highest

Tommy Robinson

40 *hate preacher:* person who encourages others to hate sb. or sth.

41 *Abu Qatada:* Islamic extremist who lives in London

48 *rally:* Kundgebung

49 *stab vest:* body protection that is used by police officers etc. to protect them from attacks using knives (or other sharp objects)

58 *Omar Bakri:* Syrian Islamic extremist who resided in Britain for many years but who is now in a Lebanese prison

59 *Al-Muhajiroun:* Islamic organization that supported terrorist activities

74 *Bury Park:* area of Luton with a large Muslim population

rates of teen pregnancy, and that's because of the way women are allowed to dress. All of this would end under Sharia law. Islam is what this country needs, people just don't realise it yet.

[...] Robinson and Saiful have much more in common than they would dare admit – both are blinded by their hatred for another's way of life. Neither will open their minds to the idea of co-existing or working to restore harmony.

In a year when Luton is bidding for city status, it is their feuding that continues to characterise this once vibrant and tightly knit community.

People in Luton hit back at extremists for damaging the town's image – and hailed it a peaceful area in which to live.

Akbar Dad Khan said: 'These people represent a tiny minority on both sides. They do not represent Luton and they damage its reputation.

The former cabbie added: 'The town needs positive news to encourage businesses to get the economy growing again.'

Akbar, 59, who works in the community and is a member of the anti-racist group Building Bridges, said: 'Luton is a town where people co-exist peacefully and harmoniously. The Muslim community has integrated into the town and plays its part. Mr Robinson says he has read the Koran but puts his own interpretation on it. Islam is a peaceful religion. The vast majority of people from all backgrounds are tolerant. It is wrong to pick out Luton as some hotbed of terrorism. Saiful Islam does not reflect the views of the Muslim community – only his own.'

Mum-of-three Marie Gildea, 46, a receptionist, said extremists spoke solely for themselves.

She added: 'Extremists from both sides are not good for Luton's image. They are a small number of people who give the town a bad name. The vast majority don't share their views. I've lived in Luton all my life. It is a good place to live and has a lot going for it. If you make the effort to mix with your neighbours you all get on. That is what most of us do. TV shows like tonight's give a false impression and make the town look bad.'

Saiful Islam

94 *bid for city status:* apply to become a city
95 *feud* [fju:d]: fight, argue
96 *tightly knit:* very close
103 *cabbie (infml):* taxi driver

1 Divide into two groups, with one group writing a profile of Tommy Robinson and one of Saiful Islam. In your profile include information about them, what they want and what they see as being wrong with present-day Britain.

2 Write a letter to *The Sun* commenting on the article.

6 Speech Following the Terrorist Attacks in London

KEN LIVINGSTONE

On 7 July 2005 four young British Muslims detonated bombs on the public transport system in four different places in central London killing 52 people as well as themselves. The mayor of London at the time, Ken Livingstone, gave this address on hearing of the attacks.

This was a cowardly attack, which has resulted in injury and loss of life. Our thoughts are with everyone who has been injured, or lost loved ones. I want to thank the emergency services for the way they have responded.

Following the al-Qaeda attacks on September 11th in America we conducted a series of exercises in London in order to be prepared for just such an attack. One of the exercises undertaken by the government, my office and the emergency and security services was based on the possibility of multiple explosions on the transport system during the Friday rush hour. The plan that came out of that exercise is being executed today, with remarkable efficiency and courage, and I praise those staff who are involved.

I'd like to thank Londoners for the calm way in which they have responded to this cowardly attack and echo the advice of the Metropolitan Police Commissioner Sir Ian Blair – do everything possible to assist the police and take the advice of the police about getting home today. […]

I want to say one thing specifically to the world today. This was not a terrorist attack against the mighty and the powerful. It was not aimed at Presidents or Prime Ministers. It was aimed at ordinary, working-class Londoners, black and white, Muslim and Christian, Hindu and Jew, young and old. It was an indiscriminate attempt to slaughter, irrespective of any considerations for age, for class, for religion, or whatever.

That isn't an ideology, it isn't even a perverted faith – it is just an indiscriminate attempt at mass murder and we know what the objective is. They seek to divide Londoners. They seek to turn Londoners against each other. I said yesterday to the International Olympic Committee, that the city of London is the greatest in the world, because everybody lives side by side in harmony. Londoners will not be divided by this cowardly attack. They will stand together in solidarity alongside those who have been injured and those who have been bereaved and that is why I'm proud to be the mayor of that city.

Finally, I wish to speak directly to those who came to London today to take life.

I know that you personally do not fear giving up your own life in order to take others – that is why you are so dangerous. But I know you fear that you may fail in your long-term objective to destroy our free society and I can show you why you will fail.

In the days that follow look at our airports, look at our sea ports and look at our railway stations and, even after your cowardly attack, you will

1 *cowardly:* feige
20 *indiscriminate:* wahllos
20 *slaughter* [ˈslɔːtə]: kill
29 *bereaved* [bɪˈriːvd]: having lost sb. you love

SPEECH FOLLOWING THE TERRORIST ATTACKS IN LONDON

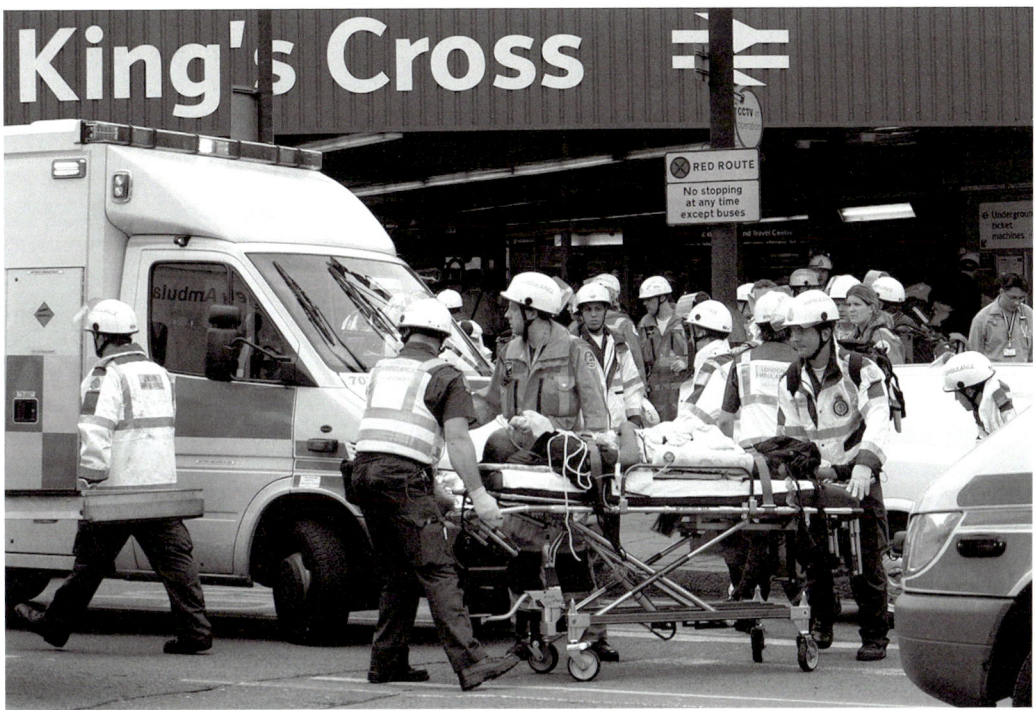

One of the injured being carried away from King's Cross underground station

see that people from the rest of Britain, people from around the world will arrive in London to become Londoners and to fulfil their dreams and achieve their potential.

They choose to come to London, as so many have come before because they come to be free, they come to live the life they choose, they come to be able to be themselves. They flee you because you tell them how they should live. They don't want that and nothing you do, however many of us you kill, will stop that flight to our city where freedom is strong and where people can live in harmony with one another. Whatever you do, however many you kill, you will fail.

44 *flee sb.:* run away from sb.

1 State which three groups of people the Mayor of London addresses in his speech, and what he says to each of them.

2 Do research on the 7 July bombings and present your findings to class.

3 Imagine that Ali has broken off all contact with his father, and that Parvez and Bettina are together when they hear of the bombings by the Islamists. Write their dialogue.

7 Oppressive or Empowering?

EVE AHMED

In this article in The Daily Mail, *Eve Ahmed examines her reaction as a woman to Islam as compared to women who have converted to Islam.*

Much of my childhood was spent trying to escape Islam. Born in London to an English mother and a Pakistani Muslim father, I was brought up to follow my father's faith without question. But, privately, I hated it. The minute I left home for university at the age of 18, I abandoned it altogether.
5 As far as I was concerned, being a Muslim meant hearing the word 'No' over and over again.

Girls from my background were barred from so many of the things my English friends took for granted. Indeed, it seemed to me that almost anything fun was haram, or forbidden, to girls like me. There were so many
10 random, petty rules. No whistling. No chewing of gum. No riding bikes. No watching *Top Of The Pops*. No wearing make-up or clothes which revealed the shape of the body. No eating in the street or putting my hands in my pockets. No cutting my hair or painting my nails. No asking questions or answering back. No keeping dogs as pets, (they were unclean). And, of
15 course, no sitting next to men, shaking their hands or even making eye contact with them. These ground rules were imposed by my father and I, therefore, assumed they must be an integral part of being a good Muslim.

Small wonder, then, that as soon as I was old enough to exert my independence, I rejected the whole package and turned my back on Islam.
20 After all, what modern, liberated British woman would choose to live such a life? Well, quite a lot, it turns out […]. And after my own break with my past, I've followed with fascination the growing trend of Western women choosing to convert to Islam. […] How, I wondered, could women be drawn to a religion which I felt had kept me in such a lowly, submissive place?
25 How could their experiences of Islam be so very different to mine?

According to Kevin Brice from Swansea University, who has specialised in studying white conversion to Islam, these women are part of an intriguing trend. He explains: 'They seek spirituality, a higher meaning, and tend to be deep thinkers. The other type of women who turn to Islam are
30 what I call "converts of convenience". They'll assume the trappings of the religion to please their Muslim husband and his family, but won't necessarily attend mosque, pray or fast.'

I spoke to a diverse selection of white Western converts in a bid to re-examine the faith I had rejected. For a significant amount of women,
35 their first contact with Islam comes from dating a Muslim boyfriend. Lynne Ali, 31, from Dagenham in Essex, freely admits to having been 'a typical white hard-partying teenager'. She says: 'I would go out and get drunk with friends, wear tight and revealing clothing and date boys. I also worked part-time as a DJ, so I was really into the club scene. I used to pray
40 a bit as a Christian, but I used God as a sort of doctor, to fix things in my

empowering: giving sb. a feeling of power

7 *bar sb.:* stop sb. from doing sth.

9 *haram (Arabic):* thing that is not clean or decent

10 *petty:* silly

28 *intriguing:* interesting because it is unusual

30 *trappings (pl):* external things associated with sth.

38 *revealing:* (of clothes) showing more of the body than is usual

life. If anyone asked, I would've said that, generally, I was happy living life in the fast lane.'

But when she met her boyfriend, Zahid, at university, something dramatic happened. She says: 'His sister started talking to me about Islam, and it was as if everything in my life fitted into place. I think, underneath it all, I must have been searching for something, and I wasn't feeling fulfilled by my hard-drinking party lifestyle.'

Lynne converted aged 19. 'From that day, I started wearing the hijab,' she explains, 'and I now never show my hair in public. At home, I'll dress in normal Western clothes in front of my husband, but never out of the house.' [...]

Brice says, often these female converts are eager to display the visible signs of their faith – in particular the hijab – whereas many Muslim girls brought up in the faith choose not to. [...]

For some converts, Islam represents a celebration of old-fashioned family values. 'Some are drawn to the sense of belonging and of community – values which have eroded in the West,' says Haifaa Jawad, a senior lecturer at the University of Birmingham, who has studied the white conversion phenomenon.

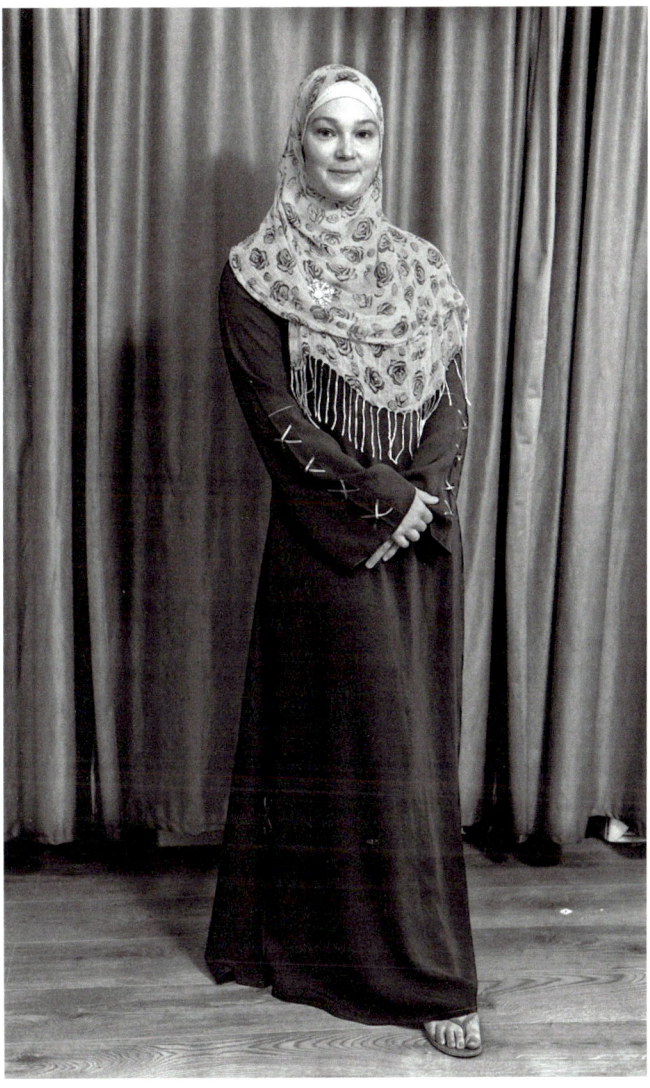

Lynne Ali in traditional Islamic dress

'Many people, from all walks of life, mourn the loss in today's society of traditional respect for the elderly and for women, for example. These are values which are enshrined in the Koran, which Muslims have to live by,' adds Brice. [...]

Several of the women I spoke to said strict Islamic dress was something they found empowering and liberating. Lynne Ali remembers the night this hit home for her. 'I went to an old friend's 21st birthday party in a bar,' she reveals. 'I walked in, wearing my hijab and modest clothing, and saw how everyone else had so much flesh on display. They were drunk, slurring their words and dancing provocatively. For the first time, I could see my former life with an outsider's eyes, and I knew I could never go back to that. I am

43 *in the fast lane:* where things are exciting and where a lot is happening

62 *eager:* wanting to do sth. very much

77 *erode:* disappear slowly

82 *mourn sth.:* feel sad about the loss of sth.

84 *enshrine sth.:* write sth. down in an important book or law

90 *slur your words:* not be able to speak clearly

OPPRESSIVE OR EMPOWERING?

so grateful I found my escape route. This is the real me – I am happy to pray five times a day and take classes at the mosque. I am no longer a slave to a broken society and its expectations.' [...]

While I don't agree with their sentiments, I admire and respect the women I interviewed for this piece. They were all bright and educated, and have thought long and hard before choosing to convert to Islam – and now feel passionately about their adopted religion. Good luck to them.

1 Compare the two women Eve Ahmed and Lynne Ali and their attitudes.

2 Explain why, like Ali in 'My Son the Fanatic', converts like 'to display the visible signs of their faith' (ll. 62–63).

3 Imagine Lynne Ali is a passenger in Parvez's taxi and attracts his curiosity due to her appearance. Write the conversation that might follow.

INFOBOX — Islam in Britain

Islam is the second largest religion in the United Kingdom: the total Muslim population is about 2.7 million, representing 4.8 % of the total population. Most Muslims live in large urban centres in England and are largely of Pakistani, Bangladeshi and Indian heritage. There is also a growing number of white British Muslims who have converted to Islam.

Although Islam, like other non-Christian religions, was made legal in 1812, the first mosque in Britain was founded in 1860 by Yemeni sailors in Cardiff. In the mid-20th century Islam became a significant religion in the UK as immigrants particularly from the Indian subcontinent moved in large numbers to Britain in search of work.

In the late 1980s that the Muslim population began to make its presence felt as a religious community rather than just a variety of ethnic communities. The event that made them noticeable was the reaction to the publication of The Satanic Verses by Salman Rushdie in 1988. The novel caused great controversy in the Islamic world. Soon after its publication, some British Muslims began to campaign against it, as they believed that the novel contained blasphemies against the founder of Islam, Mohammed. Copies of the book were burned in demonstrations in Britain. The leader of Iran, Ayatollah Khomeini issued a fatwa pronouncing a death sentence on Rushdie in February 1989, and called on Muslims all over the world to execute it. The protests brought to public attention the fact that in Britain many young Asians were turning to a particularly extreme, violent and intolerant form of Islam. Even today opinion polls indicate that many young Muslims hold more reactionary opinions than their parents, for example 36 % of young Muslims believe Muslims who convert out of Islam should be killed compared to 19 % of elderly Muslims, 74 % of young Muslims think women should wear the veil compared to 28 % of elderly Muslims.

However, the increasing fundamentalism of Muslims in the West has been part of a worldwide trend, in which political Islam and fundamentalism have been on the rise. Following the first Iraq War and the stationing of US troops on the Saudi Arabian peninsular, many Muslims have resented what they see as the intrusion of the West in the heartland of Islam. This led to the rise of Al Qaeda under Osama Bin Laden. The attacks of 11 September 2001 brought this new form of Islamic fundamentalism to world attention in a dramatic and bloody manner. A loose network of terror groups has resulted in attacks throughout the Western world, notably in London on 7 July 2005, when British Muslims committed suicide attacks on the underground system. Britain is often seen as a weak country in dealing with Islamic extremism, as many asylum seekers in Britain are extreme Islamists from Muslim countries.

While some young Muslims feel attracted to the all-embracing form of activism, other Muslims were horrified by the militant trend, feeling that their religion is being hijacked by people with a very different interpretation of Islam. Muslims tend to belong to individual mosques, so there is no single Islamic organization representing Muslims. Indeed, Muslims are very diverse in their attitudes. Only 4 % of British Muslims are Shi'a, the rest are Sunni. It is estimated that 10 % of Muslims belong to fundamentalist mosques.

ACKNOWLEDGEMENTS

Illustrations
Cover: Mosque: Tim Smith / Panos Pictures / VISU; Muslim man: London / Alamy
p. 5: andersphoto / Shutterstock.com
p. 7: Moviestore collection Ltd / Alamy
p. 10: Moviestore collection Ltd / Alamy
p. 17: R. Macdonald / REA / laif
p. 24: Bulls Press / News International
p. 25: Bulls Press / News International
p. 27: picture-alliance / dpa
p. 29: Grant Triplow / Daily Mail / Solo Syndication

Texts
1 Hanif Kureishi, 'My Son the Fanatic': First published in *The New Yorker* (1994); in book form in *Love in a Blue Time* (Faber and Faber, 1997)
2 Extremism and Muslim Extremism': From 'The Differences Between Extremists & Fanatics' and 'Beliefs of Muslim Extremists' on www.eHow.com
3 Ed Husain, 'Choosing between Family and God': From Ed Husain, *The Islamist* (London: Penguin, 2007). © Ed Husain, 2007.
4 Roger Woddis, 'Down with Fanatics': From Roger Woddis, *God's Worried* (London, New Statesman, 1983)
5 Nick Francis: 'Caught between Extremists on Both Sides': From 'Hatred tearing a town apart', *The Sun*, 27 February 2012
6 Ken Livingstone: 'Speech Following the Terrorist Attacks in London': public speech on 7 July 2005
7 Eve Ahmed: 'Oppressive or Empowering?: From 'Why are so many modern British career women converting to Islam?', *The Daily Mail*, 28 October 2010